WHAT DO DOGS DREAM ABOUT?

By Tom Kuncl
Edited by Astrid Derfler

Contents

BEST FRIENDS FOREVER

Acquiring a dog may be the only opportunity a human ever has to choose a relative.

Mordecai Siegal

How long has dog been man's – and woman's – best friend? For hundreds of centuries. Much longer than the relationship that would later develop with our other favorite pet – the cat.

Remarkable paintings of early man have been found on the walls of deep, dark caves in France, Spain and China, as well as other scattered places around the world where archaeologists are uncovering the early history of mankind.

We might say the ancient drawings are the first family "photo albums" created by the hands of humans. They are at least 10,000 years old. Among those Stone Age magic moments are pictures of – dogs!

Where did dogs come from, anyway? The first dogs – which were probably wolves – were the ancient ancestors of today's 150 breeds of modern dog to which science has given the name *Canis familiaris*, and to which we have tacked on the likes of Fido, Rover, Spot, Tootsie and Tweetie Pie, and sometimes, for snooty blue-ribboned champions, names like Percival Archibald le Beau III.

The cave-dogs are shown accompanying man on the hunt, playing alongside children and sleeping comfortably by the fire.

In some of the drawings they actually appear to be smiling. Those wolfish grins, no doubt, prompted our cave-dwelling, wall-painting ancestor – let's call him Mr. Og – to turn to Mrs. Og and say: "Is it just my imagination or does that dog look like he is laughing at me?"

It is a question Mrs. Og could not answer and one that has remained elusive and hotly debated down through the ages that followed as the dog became even closer to the human family, continuing to serve us, love us and amuse us, and – no doubt – being every bit as amused by us.

Have we learned anything since the time of the Ogs?

Do dogs smile – and if so, when and why?

Do dogs dream? And if they do – what do they dream about?

Do dogs understand what we mean when we say things to them?

Are words even necessary for them to know what we're thinking and what we're feeling?

Have those thousands of years at our sides, doing our bidding with willing hearts, created some special bond that exists between us and no other species of animal on this planet?

Or are we just being foolishly romantic in thinking so? Have we fallen into a trap that science calls anthropomorphism – the projecting of human traits onto animals when they do yet another of those amazing or unbelievable things that convinces us that they've been reading our minds?

ANIMAL OR HUMAN?

You think dogs will not be in heaven? I tell you, they will be there long before any of us.

Robert Louis Stevenson

Do dogs share some of our "human" traits?

The traditional position of science has been that because we love our dogs so much, we want to believe they possess abilities they really don't. Those same scientists in their starched white coats tell us we are wrong to apply concepts such as "think" or "plan" or "learn" when we discuss what may be going on in the minds of our pets.

Dogs, or any animal for that matter, say the scientists, may appear to be acting in some strikingly human way, but in fact they are only carrying out what science has termed a "conditioned response" to a frequently repeated message from us humans – for example, calling them by name when we wish them to come.

Yes, dogs and other animals certainly have brains, and obvious intelligence, perhaps even "minds," but not minds that parallel ours in any way.

9

Dogs only know what genetics determined they needed to know and that information was hot-wired into their brains at birth, so that theory goes. Dogs, says Mr. Scientist, don't open bank accounts because they cannot grasp the concept of saving.

Well, I then respond, what do you think they are doing when they bury bones?

But the study of animal behavior – and in particular the interaction between man and dog – has advanced incredibly in just the last two decades. Mrs. Og may not have been able to answer her husband's question, but scientists today say they believe they can at least begin to do so. Let's hear what they have to say...

Do dogs smile?

Yes, dogs smile when they're happy (and frown when they're sad or if we are sad).

Dogs grin by pulling back the corners of their lips and baring their teeth. A very relaxed dog will smile and then close his eyes.

(Don't make the mistake of confusing a grin with a snarl. If a dog has his mouth pulled back, but is showing his incisors and back teeth, most likely he's snarling.)

While we are on the subject of dogs and smiles, it is worth quoting Elizabeth Marshall Thomas who wrote the wonderful, heartwarming book *The Hidden Life of Dogs* (A Peter Davison Book, Houghton Mifflin Company, 1993):

"All dogs smile, which is to say their faces become pleasant and relaxed, with ears low, eyes half shut, lips soft and parted, and chin high. This is a dog smile.

"Yet a few dogs also emulate human smiles, and hence they themselves are anthropomorphizing. In the presence of human beings, these dogs will draw back their lips grotesquely to bare their teeth, making the same face we make. At the same time, these dogs may also roll over to reveal their bellies submissively, showing they understand exactly what our smiles mean."

Why do dogs smile?

When asked why a dog smiles, dog behaviorist Janice Falk says it's simply because they're happy!

Or perhaps, she says, it's the whole domestication process and the dog is copying human behavior. A smile consistently produced a favorable response from his owners, and therefore the smile became a part of the pet's personality.

Is there a special kind of relationship between people and dogs?

There is some special relationship between us and the dogs we love that has more to do with soul than science. A lot of what makes that relationship so special is that your dog wants – more than anything else in the world – to please his human master.

We intuitively knew that long before modern research was able to verify it and express it in words such as these from Dr. Alan Beck, a professor at Purdue University and one of the world's foremost authorities on dog behavior: "Dogs have both an intellectual and an emotional life."

"There are undoubtedly still scientists out there who question the intelligence of dogs because they don't have what they think of as hard data. They feel it's unscientific to acknowledge phenomena we can't prove. But who says we can't prove it?"

Do dogs ever get embarrassed?

Dr. Beck says you bet they do!

"I am absolutely convinced that my dog feels guilty when he wets on the rug. A blind observer could see it. He behaves the same way I would have if my mother had caught me doing it.

"If it looks the same as human behavior in the same situation and is being used to solve the same problem, why shouldn't we be able to use words we use for human emotions to describe it?" Dr. Beck asks.

"There truly is a special bond between ourselves and dogs, and we are coming to a much better understanding of it today than ever before. They are an important part of our lives and we are an important part of theirs, and we are both the better for it," the researcher adds.

Can dogs think?

Melissa Miller, author of the best-selling book *The Dog IQ Test for Dogs and Owners* (Penguin, 1994), says those who think that dogs don't know how to think and reason are too stubborn to acknowledge the evidence that exists and the experiences that almost every dog owner has shared in some way:

"Think about what happens when you take your suitcases out of the closet. I'll bet that your dog displays a reaction. He makes the association between those suitcases and the fact that you are planning to leave to go someplace without him. That takes an ability to reason," Miller says, then adds:

"Look at guide dogs for the blind who learn what is called 'intelligent disobedience.'

"These dogs take it upon themselves to disobey the owner's command if carrying out that command would be dangerous to their master based on information the dog can assess but the master can't. Even though they want to please their master more than anything in the world, they'll disobey."

Do dogs dream?

Yes, dogs dream, and while they aren't able to bore us with the details (as some of our other friends will), scientists are beginning to come up with a pretty good idea of what they're dreaming about.

But, says Dr. Randy Lockwood, a behavior specialist for the American Humane Society, we still don't know as much about that as we would like.

Science hasn't been too motivated so far to find out what dogs dream, but there's no doubt that they do — and they seem to enjoy it.

"Anyone who has watched a dog taking a nap is certain to have seen what clearly appears to be dream activity going on. That has been confirmed in the laboratory. Dogs do dream as measured by brain wave activity.

"We can observe them at home twitching and moving their paws in a kind of sleeping/running motion and it isn't hard to imagine that the content of their dream involves some kind of activity. It isn't too far off the wall to assume that some of those dreams might be enjoyable to them just as ours are," Dr. Lockwood says.

At the University of Virginia Medical School Sleep and Dream Laboratory, professor emeritus Robert Van de Castle has studied human and animal dreams for more than 30 years. He concludes that dogs do dream, but differently than humans.

What do dogs dream about?

"Dogs probably just review things that have happened during the day and relive some exciting experience. You can see them twitch their tail or hear them growl as they review something that has happened, but I don't believe they will come up with some way to make things happen better as a result of dreaming or be able to put closure on some situation in the way humans are able," Dr. Van de Castle believes.

However, other researchers believe dog dreams may be more important than scientists are now able to prove.

14

"We come back to the basic problem of trying to re-late to some animal activity in terms which we can re-late to rather than perceiving it from the animal point of view," says Dr. Beck.

"When and if we are able to understand things from a dog's point of view, we may discover that dogs have a dream life every bit as significant as our own and one that serves some very useful purpose to them," he adds.

Do dogs have a sense of humor?

Dr. Lockwood thinks they do.

"There is no animal that is more willing to be play-ful with us than the dog. Much of that play is the kind that makes us laugh – chasing a ball and doing all of the silly things we see our dogs do," Dr. Lockwood says.

"They know that we find these things funny – they can hear us laughing – and they repeat the thing that cracked us up. Just in terms of pure observation, you would have to say they understand the concept of humor and get the same kick out of it that we do.

"That mischievous side is something most dog own-ers know about first hand. A good example of this is recounted by *Time* magazine writer Michael Lemonick:

"I once knew a golden retriever named Newton who had a perverse sense of humor. Whenever I tossed a Frisbee for him to chase, he'd take off in hot pursuit but then seemed to lose track of it.

"Trotting back and forth only a yard or two from the toy, Newton would look all around, even up into the trees. He seemed genuinely baffled.

"Finally, I'd give up and head into the field to help him out. But no sooner would I get within 10 feet of him than he would invariably dash straight over to the Frisbee, grab it and start running like mad, looking over his shoulder with what looked suspiciously like a grin."

How else do dogs communicate?

Smiling isn't the only tool which dogs rely on to communicate, says one of America's most widely known animal experts, columnist and author Dr. Michael Fox. "Dogs express themselves in ways that are quite similar to humans," Fox says.

"Both dogs and humans growl when angry, whimper when hurt and whine when unhappy or disappointed. We both stare directly at someone we wish to challenge and grin at someone we are happy to see.

"Dogs also have an open-mouth 'play face' expression, often accompanied by panting, which is the equivalent of human laughter," Dr. Fox says.

Can dogs fall in love?

Psychologist Frank Beach once did an unusual series of experiments with beagles while he was professor of psychology at the University of California.

Beach raised females and then allowed them to meet and get friendly with male beagles as they prepared to come into a mating cycle. In test after test the females picked out the same favorite mate and demonstrated to Dr. Beach what certainly looked like love to him:

"If someone will explain human love to me, then I could compare it to what I see in my dogs," Dr. Beach said.

Can dogs talk?

Of course. The "language" dogs speak to us can't be written, but it certainly can be understood, says Dr. Fox:

"An aggressive dog will stare at you squarely, snarl and wag a stiff tail. A fearful dog will go on the defensive by shifting his body weight backward and lowering his tail. A dog that wants to show complete submission will curl up with ears flattened against his head and remain cowering or completely still on the ground," Dr. Fox says.

Some dogs even express their personality by the way they carry their body, says Dr. Lockwood of the American Humane Society:

"You'll see some dogs who actually seem to be strutting, full of life and confidence with tails and ears erect. Then you'll see others who are kind of slinking around – with what you might call a hang-dog look. That's something they learn in their home environment. They are often pretty good mirrors of their master or mistress," Dr. Lockwood says.

Dogs use their tails and ears to signal us – and other dogs – things that are on their minds.

"Many people mistake all tail wagging as friendly, but it's not. When the tail is high and wagging stiffly, a dog is telling you that he is making a judgment about you and the situation, and could be getting angry," Dr. Lockwood says. "The tail low to the ground and rapid wagging is one of the signs by which they signal their friendly intentions," he adds.

A sure sign that your dog wants to play is an easily recognized posture in which he seems to stretch his forepaws leisurely, execute a little bow and raise one front paw. The same signal for play is observed among wolf packs in the wild.

What is my dog saying?

Dogs "talk" to us in a variety of ways, and if we're willing to listen and learn, we can "talk" right back to them.

"Hi, I'm glad to see you!" This bark is high-pitched, repeated and is followed with lots of tail-wagging and grinning. You probably already know this greeting. It's the one your pet uses when you come home from work.

"Will you play with me?" When your pup wants to play, he'll lower his two front paws, put his chest down to the ground, flatten his ears and lift his rear end in the air. Dog behaviorists call this the "play bow," and no one who sees it is able to resist it.

"Stay away!" A dog warns you of possible danger with a series of low-pitched, frenzied

barks that should have you up and investigating immediately.

"Something's wrong!"

This type of warning bark is usually accompanied by growling, raised hair on the neck and flattened ears.

"I'm scared!"

A scared dog crouches low to the floor, with his head down and ears flat. If he barks at all, it will be an odd sounding, howl-type bark.

"I'm very sad"

We've all heard the expression "puppy dog eyes." There's nothing more heart-wrenching than the sight of those downcast eyes and drooping ears that a dog demonstrates when he's not happy.

If your dog is feeling especially unhappy, he may howl. This dog needs attention and a big hug.

"I love you!"

This is the type of "dog-talk" all dog lovers live for. You know it's puppy love when you are greeted with lots of face licking and tail wagging.

Wolves in packs use face licking as a sign of affection and trust. When your dog drags his tongue across your face, take it as a compliment and consider yourself one lucky person.

Are there IQ tests for dogs?

Highly complicated testing of dog "intelligence" has taken place at animal medical teaching centers around the world. Interpreting the results does not yet end the argument between those who believe in dogs as fully equipped emotional beings and those who remain in the trenches of earlier belief.

"What we know for certain is that a dog is very smart at being a dog and a cat is very smart at being a cat and that both of them have communication skills that allow them to 'talk' among themselves. New ways are being identified that allow us to not just eavesdrop on them, but to communicate with them ourselves based on new understandings of the similarities between them and us," says Dr. Randy Lockwood.

A sign of the times...

Here's a little tidbit from *Woman's World* magazine (January 3, 1995) about a dog that really knew how to listen.

Dog owners Bill and Elizabeth Hagee adopted a deaf puppy born of their daughter Cynthia's dog. How, they wondered, could they train a pet that couldn't hear? They finally took the pup named Sparky to a trainer who taught deaf dogs. Sparky soon became the star student by learning different hand signals.

By watching both the trainer, Berta Nielsen, and the other dogs in the class, little Sparky learned sign language.

Have dogs changed much in the last few thousand years?

To learn more about what makes a dog tick, researchers study packs of wild wolves. Studying wolves as they live in the wild has given dog behavior experts many clues about how dogs think, how they communicate, and how we can achieve a better relationship with our pets.

Dr. Peter Borchelt, animal behavior therapist at New York City's Animal Medical Center, provides this important insight:

"Dogs, like wolves, think as 'pack' animals and as a result are accustomed to following orders from a leader in the pack. In our homes, the dog anticipates that we are the leader of that 'pack' and is ready to do most of what we ask if we ask it in the right way," Borchelt says.

What's the best way to teach my dog to obey commands?

Bashkin Dibra, author of the highly popular *Dog Training by Bash* (Dutton, 1992), says that today's dogs retain a memory of the ancient codes they needed for survival and are still profoundly guided by them.

"Everything the dog does, all his needs, are related to the hierarchy of the wolf pack. When he looks at you he is waiting for you to show him you are boss – the pack leader," Dibra says. "He's telling you to please punch in the right codes. 'I love to do what I have to do, but if you don't show me, I'm confused.'

"Your dog will understand and learn what you want him to learn when you use a deep, deliberate tone of voice when giving a command or scolding. The command should be given once, briefly, such as 'Come!' or 'Sit!' or Stay!'" Dibra says. "Never whine or plead or nag. It will only confuse the animal."

The knowledge gained from wolf research is also applied by Liz Gordon, founder of Citydog Obedience School in New York City, who echoes Dibra about communicating with your dog:

"Someone needs to be in charge, and if you don't tell them what to do, they'll tell you," Gordon says.

When dogs and their masters have problems, it generally isn't because the dog is unwilling, but because the human has failed to get the right message across, says veterinarian Dr. Paul Constantino. "People think smelly old sneakers make great toys, then turn around and have a fit when the dog chews on their brand new sneakers," Dr. Constantino says.

"Really, why should dogs discriminate between old shoes and new ones?"

Hey, why are dogs known as "man's" best friend?

The very special bond between women and dogs was explored in a unique study conducted at State University of New York and later reported on in the *Journal of Personality and Social Psychology*. The study proved beyond a doubt that dogs certainly aren't only man's best friend (not that we believed that anyway).

In this study, 45 women who owned or liked dogs were broken into three separate groups and asked to perform a number of tricky mathematical computations. One group was required to complete the test under the clearly stressful eye of a researcher who seemed to be waiting to catch them in a mistake.

The second group wrestled with the math problems with a researcher present, but also with a friend who accompanied them to lend moral support.

The third group of volunteers were also monitored by a researcher, but were allowed to bring their dogs into the room.

Throughout the test, the blood pressure and pulse of the women were checked, along with the amount of perspiring, if any, that the stressful situation provoked.

When the results were studied and compared, the women who had their faithful four-footed companions at their side displayed dramatically lower levels of blood pressure and pulse rate, and hardly put their antiperspirant to work at all. Not only that, the group with their dogs did remarkably better with the math problems.

Researchers described the results this way: "The presence of dogs during the performance of the stressful task provided the kind of non-evaluative social support that is critical to buffering physiological responses to acute stress." Translated to everyday English that means: "It felt good to have my best friend around to help."

What else are scientists discovering about our relationships with dogs?

Interesting side notes were collected by the researchers who conducted this study. They interviewed the women especially close to their dogs regarding their attitude toward the dogs. Among the responses were clear indications that a kind of love existed between mistress and pet that had a meaning all its own:

"They described the relations they had with their dogs as special and different from all other relationships," the researchers reported.

"Several divorced women said that whereas husbands may come and go and children may grow up and leave home, a dog is forever.

"We were told that dogs never withhold their love, they never get angry and leave and they never go out looking for new owners," the report concluded.

Why – and how – does owning a dog keep us healthy?

H. Jon Geis, Ph.D., a clinical psychologist in New York, says it results in part from what he believes is "a truly and total loving relationship in which we feel intimately involved and in return feel safe and cared for by our animal companion."

Dr. Leo Bustad, a veterinarian who is president of a group called Delta Society that promotes animal-human connections, puts it this way:

"A dog can be a wonderful cheerleader. They can buoy our spirits and help banish depressing thoughts.

"They can distract us from our worries, make us feel more secure and motivate us to exercise.

"Most importantly, they are a great source of fun and laughter, and more studies are showing that humor is a powerful tool in reducing stress," Dr. Bustad says.

The point that Dr. Bustad raises about dogs encouraging us to exercise – another healthy habit – was supported in a study reported in 1991 in the *British Journal of the Royal Society of Medicine.*

Dog owners took more frequent and longer walks than people with any other kind of pet and substantially more than people who had no pet at all. The result was that they had fewer health problems over the period in which the study was conducted.

Author and researcher Dr. Janet Rucker – whose book *The Four-Footed Therapist* (Dutton, 1992) states that pets are mental health counselors who don't charge fees – says that one of the best "prescriptions" a doctor could write for a patient complaining of tension, anxiety, fatigue and depression would be a map showing him or her how to get to the nearest pet store or animal shelter to obtain a new friend.

"Watching, stroking, playing with or talking to your pet has an immediate beneficial effect on your body," Dr. Rucker says.

"Just being with your pet reduces blood pressure and lowers anxiety."

Would you buy a used car from a man with a dog?

Here is another benefit dog owners have over the rest of the population: People think more highly of you if you're a dog owner, a recent study showed.

Persons were given photos to view that included men and women, some of whom were depicted with dogs at their sides and some of whom were not.

The test subjects were then asked to form an opinion of the people based solely on the pictures. Almost everyone said the people who were shown with dogs appeared to be the trustworthy, honest type. They also speculated that those with a dog at their side were happier and more relaxed than the others.

In a similar experiment, students walked through a park, first accompanied by a friendly looking dog on a leash and then just by themselves.

Their assignment was to try to strike up conversations with strangers. Again, the results were dramatic. People paused to respond to the students walking the dogs. Many reached down to pet the animals and comment upon them.

Professor Andrew Rowan, director of Boston's Tufts University Center for Animals and Public Policy, made this observation about those studies:

"Dogs convey an image of trust. That's why almost all politicians make sure they are photographed with dogs."

Those studies attracted the close attention of the people who sell us products – not just for dogs – but products for humans, too.

Some night while watching television, count the number of times you see a commercial that includes a dog. You'll be astonished and you'll get the idea, too. The manufacturer wants you to think of them as trustworthy and friendly – just like the folks in the photos!

DR. DOG... GOOD FOR HEART AND SOUL

Old age means realizing you will never own all the dogs you wanted to.

Joe Gores

Can dogs help us live longer?

It might strike us as a little funny at first, bringing to mind a picture of our pup dressed up in a little doctor or nurse outfit, clucking sympathetically and expertly diagnosing us as we sniffle and sneeze our way through a cold, face a mountain of bills or find ourselves wondering whether or not that certain someone truly cares about us.

Doesn't it always seem to us that, somehow, our

best friend appears to understand and wants to share our burden?

Haven't we all seen that special look in their eyes, that wag of the tail that's as impish as a wink, the gentle paw on our knee at just the right moment, the head cocked as if to ask us if everything is OK or one of those smiles we now know REALLY IS A SMILE and an invitation to forget – even if just for a bit – whatever it is that ails us and enjoy the genuine love they clearly know we need?

If all we could rely upon was our own experience that dogs are wondrous healers of the things that wound and worry us – body and spirit – that they are a medicine as beneficial as any created in the laboratories of science, for most of us, our own experiences would be proof enough of that truth.

But science has known for ages that dogs are good *to* us and *for* us in ways that go far beyond the routine kinds of things we've asked them to do.

In the past few years, numerous studies and careful research has shown, beyond any doubt, that our friend the dog helps keep us healthy, physically and emotionally and, in fact, has brought incredible healings in situations where all other medicines had failed to work.

Can dogs help kids get better, too?

On a later page of this book you will read about an amazing dog named Mirko who was trained to visit with desperately ill kids in a Texas children's hospital.

Time after time, the gentle giant Mirko broke through the walls of silence the dying children had built around themselves, calming the children so completely they became willing to take treatments they had struggled against before. The children would endure the treatments to please their friend Mirko when he "asked" in a language that only the kids and the dog seemed to understand.

In Ft. Collins, Colorado, special education teachers had exhausted every advanced educational theory and technique they could find in hopes of reaching a desperately withdrawn autistic girl whom they were trying to teach how to read – with no luck.

At the suggestion of another teacher, a romping and fun-loving big black Labrador named Ashleigh was introduced into the classroom environment.

The teachers still do not know why Ashleigh chose the self-imprisoned girl to be the special recipient of her attention, but she did.

Within weeks, the silent child began trying to form words from the pages of the books she had once refused to open. As time went on, there came one memorable day... the moment in which she settled in  a corner with Ashleigh and began reading aloud stories that made her and the old dog smile and laugh together in sheer delight as the teachers looked on with tears in their eyes.

What does science say about all this?

In hospitals, nursing homes and hospices across America today, dogs are brightening the lives of the terminally ill, the mentally ill and the seriously depressed and lonely.

At the Elmhurst Extended Care Facility in Providence, Rhode Island, the nursing staff tells the story of an elderly woman patient who had no living relatives to visit her. She was becoming even further isolated by her progressive deafness, but stubbornly refused to be examined and fitted for a hearing aid.

That was before she met a big collie that was brought to the home by volunteers taking part in a project to match up the elderly with pets. This was a very understanding and wise collie who made it a point to become her special friend.

"Now she has gone and gotten a hearing aid and she just loves to show off HER dog to the other residents," reported Audrey Dupont, the center's activities director.

The elderly who are self-sufficient and able to take care of themselves and share their home with a dog owe some of that freedom to that companionship, according to an impressive study conducted by University of California epidemiologist Dr. Judith Siegel.

In research designed to measure the amount of stress going on in the lives of 1,000 Medicare recipients and how often they visited a doctor for relief of their symptoms, Dr. Siegel made some interesting discoveries:

The 40 percent of the study group of elderly who

had pets – mostly dogs – sought the services of a doctor far less often than those who had no animal companions.

Even more surprising, it did not matter what medical condition they were suffering from or how serious the medical condition was – those who had dogs for friends seemed dramatically less prone to seek medical care, especially the kind that really wasn't necessary.

The research proved the theory that many doctors who treat the elderly have – that the purpose of their visits and often the symptoms they complained of were not very serious and the reason they wanted to see the doctor was because they were lonely and therefore imagined their aches and pains.

One major conclusion drawn from Dr. Siegel's research was that the company of a pet reduced the need for the elderly to seek the attention of the health-care system.

Another benefit was surprising, too. Dogs owners do not often fall into the depression that strikes many elderly people when a friend, relative or loved one becomes seriously ill or dies. The friendship of their pet acts as what Dr. Siegel described as a "stress buffer" in those situations.

A study aimed at determining the value of pets in reducing depression among the elderly was conducted by University of Kentucky School of Medicine researcher Dr. Thomas Garrity. The results again showed that pet owners were better able to adjust to the death of a spouse than those people who had no pet to look to for solace.

But it's not just the elderly for whom tests have proven that dogs work health wonders...

Could Fido be a cardiologist?

Why not? We know what big hearts our canine friends have.

Research by Erika Friedman of Brooklyn College shows that animal companionship increased the survival rate of heart attack victims of all ages.

In a similar study, the recovery rates of 92 men who had suffered heart attacks were followed for one year. Those who had pets had a much more successful recovery than those who had no connection to an animal friend.

Results of that study, published by the U.S. Department of Public Health, concluded: "Only three out of 53 patients with pets died, whereas 11 out of 39 patients without pets expired."

In 1992, researchers in Melbourne, Australia, conducted what is perhaps the largest and one of the most dramatic studies of the relationship between cardiac health and owning a dog or similar responsive pet.

Of nearly 6,000 volunteers who were screened for common conditions associated with cardiac problems, 15 percent who owned dogs proved to have much fewer of the predictors of heart disease, such as high blood pressure or elevated cholesterol levels.

Those differences were observed regardless of other lifestyle and habit patterns of those studied including diet, exercise or smoking. More surprising yet, the pet owners proved to be among some of the worst in terms of choosing heart-healthy meals. Many, it was discovered, were frequent fast-food diners and all consumed meats at higher volumes than the average of the test group.

Can dogs help arthritis sufferers?

Even the crippling disease of arthritis may be relieved by our friendship with dogs, say medical experts like Dr. Dan Lago, a specialist in gerontology at Pennsylvania State University. Dr. Lago believes dogs give arthritis victims a motive to be more active than they might otherwise be and that the additional activity helps slow the progress of the arthritis.

"If they have a difficult time getting up in the morning and starting their routine, the need to care for a pet can be a great incentive," Dr. Lago says.

Just as importantly, the physician adds, is that having a pet they know depends upon them gives the arthritic sufferer a sense of self-esteem. In arthritis patients without pets, self-esteem diminishes as the effects of the disease advance and they are able to do less for themselves.

So convinced is Dr. Lago that arthritis victims can be helped by dogs, that he heads a volunteer group called PACT (People and Animals Coming Together) that matches up homeless dogs and cats with senior citizens. The group provides ongoing help while the elderly and their pet get to know and care for each other.

Dr. Lago remembers one of many success stories of the joining together of seniors and pets: An elderly woman fell while hanging up clothes on an outside wash line. She was unable to summon aid with her cries for help. But when her new dog-friend, Jody, barked up a storm, a passerby stopped and came to the woman's rescue.

Dogs who guide the blind and deaf are common sights now. But just emerging on the scene are those patient, sweet-natured dogs who have been trained to walk at the side of cerebral palsy victims, planting their four feet firmly and permitting their sometimes trembling master or mistress to steady themselves against their sturdy frames.

Can dogs detect cancer?

One of the strangest examples of the usefulness of dogs in human medicine was a recent discovery in London which resulted from an elderly woman's trust in her pet's intuition.

As reported in medical journals there, the woman

at first became annoyed when her pet continually sniffed at a mole she'd had on her leg for years and to which her dog had paid no previous attention. When nothing would stop the animal from his constant interest in the mole, a local vet to whom she took the pet at last suggested perhaps she should have the skin lesion checked by her doctor to try to determine what had made it so interesting to the dog.

On examination, the mole proved to be a deadly malignant melanoma. Surgery was performed and the woman experienced a normal recovery, but doctors were baffled by the dog's uncanny actions.

Research prompted by their curiosity led to the discovery that a specific protein that develops in melanoma tissue gives off an odor that humans cannot detect, but dogs can. All the implications of that finding are not clear, but for the lady in London, a dog's wet nose proved to be a medical tool that may have saved her life.

KEEPING YOUR DOG IN TIP-TOP SHAPE

Dogs laugh, but they laugh with their tails.

Max Eastman

How good is America's dog health care system?

Since we now know that our dog-friends are such good medicine for us, we must return the favor in kind – and it seems that we do.

No nation spends more on the health care of its dogs – and other pets – than Americans. The figure is now close to $10 billion annually, according to the Veterinary Medical Association (VMA).

And the medical care doctors are now able to provide for our aging or injured pets has become almost miraculous. There are very few advanced procedures used to treat human illness or accident that are not also available to our dogs at neighborhood animal clinics and at university teaching schools, where every tool of modern medical science is used on behalf of our friends.

CAT scans (you needn't tell your dog that's what they're called!) and other sophisticated tests detect early forms of cancers that threaten the life of dogs. A wide range of chemotherapy can then be used to save their lives.

Pacemaker implants have become fairly routine, as has prosthetic hip surgery, plastic surgery, hearing aids and organ transplants, and even dental root canals are part of the medical wonders available for dogs and our other pets.

The veterinarians who now perform these lifesaving procedures for dogs are quick to point out that there is a touching trace of irony in our use of these treatments which extend the lives of our friends. Many of the incredible techniques that now save both human and animal lives were learned by first testing the techniques on animals.

Those state-of-the-art treatments have become more and more commonplace at busy metropolitan animal clinics. At the Niles Animal Hospital in suburban Chicago, skilled veterinarians routinely perform blood cell counts, biopsies and the complicated removal of malignant or otherwise threatening tumors.

The ECG – which is used to assess heart health – is now available nationwide through an ingenious bit of technology offered by a New York firm called Cardiopet. This company markets a transmitter that small-town vets can use to send an ECG for analysis by phone to the company's data center.

Then at the center, highly trained veterinary cardiologists examine the ECG reading and recommend treatment for the individual dog. That same innovative company recently developed a method through which X-ray pictures can also be sent via phone line and similar services provided.

While many new types of equipment have been designed especially for the diagnosis and treatment of dogs, a great deal of the technology now available for use by animal doctors is the same as a well-equipped human hospital would use in the treatment of us.

Some of the more advanced devices, in fact, are second-hand equipment bought from "people" hospitals. Small adjustments need to be made because dog tissue is more easily scanned than human, but the miraculous result is the same – our dogs are examined with the same technologies which we've come to count on to keep us well.

Here's a weird footnote on the subject of using human medical practices on dogs:

Recently, there was a brouhaha in London dog-fancier circles. A sad-faced bloodhound was disqualified from competition because judges charged that plastic surgery had been performed to improve the dog's looks.

Are dogs living longer?

Ironically, because we take such good care of our pets – getting them to the veterinarian more often and treating them with effective antibiotics for a host of ailments that once shortened their lives – our dogs are living much longer. Consequently, they are suffering from many of the diseases of advancing years that also affect us humans.

Do you think of your dog as a real family member?

There is another reason we are willing to pay for sometimes very expensive medical treatment for our dogs, according to research cited by Dr. Aaron Katcher of the University of Pennsylvania's Center for the Interaction of Animals and Society:

"More people today think of their dog and other pets as an actual member of the family," Dr. Katcher says.

In recent surveys, the percentage of pet owners who think of their dog as pretty much human, has grown from about 49 percent 20 years ago to nearly 80 percent today.

Dr. Katcher says it is the overall decentralization of today's American family life that has caused us to form deeper bonds with our pets. When they become sick, we want them well again and hang the cost.

"If you walk into a veterinary hospital today, you can't tell from listening to the conversations whether they're talking about humans or animals," says the researcher. At the university hospital with which he is associated, social workers counsel pet owners whose animals are being treated for cancer.

Among the gifts they bring to us in our sometimes rootless-seeming society is a sense that we are needed – and we are loved without reservation, according to research done by Dr. Katcher and another prominent researcher, Dr. Alan Beck who now heads the Center for Applied Ethology and Human-Animal Interaction at the Purdue University School of Veterinary Medicine.

In detailed studies done by Drs. Beck and Katcher,

evidence shows how dogs bring another bag of beneficial feelings to some lonely homes.

"They sometimes fill the role an infant or small child once filled in a household, particularly for the elderly whose children are gone now and living at distances," Dr. Beck says.

For those people who have that happy desire accommodated by a dog or other pet, their attitudes toward it take on dimensions that are almost totally similar to the interaction between a parent and a child, according to that research.

"People talk to their pets as if they were children, and even pause as they're speaking as if they are waiting for a reply. That reply can only be an expression on the dog's face, but it is communication of a kind that satisfies both the pet owner and the pet," Dr. Beck says.

Another small bit of magic was observed as the researchers observed people sharing those deep kinds of feelings with their dogs:

"The person's face would actually soften very frequently, seeming to release the stress and anxiety that was apparent before.

"Dogs have a wonderful capacity to give that sort of feeling to many people who find it difficult to satisfy that need in other ways they may no longer have access to," the Purdue researcher notes.

That health benefit to humans study conducted by Dr. Siegel in California underscored those comforting gifts dogs bring to humans. A striking percentage of those asked how they thought their pet felt about them responded that they believed their dogs loved them as much as they loved their dogs.

MORE BIZARRE "TAILS"

Some of our greatest historical and artistic treasures we place in museums; others we take for walks.

Roger A. Caras

Are dogs psychic?

If we believe that our dogs are aware of our feelings at the very deepest level, is it too hard to take an additional step and consider the possibility that they – like some humans – have other special abilities that go much further beyond our understanding?

Could it be that our dogs are psychic? There are many experts who believe just that. They have collected a large body of evidence to back up their claim – which no longer seems to be quite so out of the question as it once was.

Author Bill Shull has collected numerous stories of dogs that seemed to possess amazing powers of extra-

43

sensory perception – ESP. In his unusual and interesting book, *Animal Immortality* (Fawcett, 1991), Shull tells the story of a woman named Welcome Lewis who, while visiting San Francisco, decided to take a walk in that city's Lafayette Park with her normally enthusiastic companion, a small boxer.

After finding a parking place, the woman was surprised – and annoyed – when her pet steadfastly refused to get out of the car. Finally giving up in anger and disgust, she drove back to the hotel where she was staying, scolding her strangely stubborn pet all the way.

The next day, however, as the woman drove past the park, she gasped in horror when she saw that a giant tree had fallen onto the exact spot where her car had been parked. Upon asking, she learned that it had crashed to earth only minutes after she and her psychic pooch had pulled away.

Jaytee –
One Smart Dog

Another dog with an unexplainable sixth sense has been the subject of many highly controlled scientific tests in Lancashire, England. The studies were conducted by widely respected biologist Dr. Rupert Sheldrake.

For months, a tiny terrier named Jaytee had been warmly surprising his mistress, Pam Smart, by waiting, ears perked and tail wagging, in a window of the home they shared.

The owner quite logically assumed the dog had become accustomed to her fairly regular arrival time and gave it little attention until she became unemployed and began coming home at widely different hours. To her amazement, she discovered that Jaytee always knew when she was on her way home and waited, perched in his favorite greeting place.

The unusual story made its way to Dr. Sheldrake and a test of the dog's actions was prepared. One camera crew set up at Smart's home, and filmed Jaytee's routine.

Another crew followed Smart – just to make certain there was no tip-off about her movements – such as a ringing phone the woman might have used to alert the dog she was on her way.

At four different times over the course of several days – the times selected at random – Smart was told to head for her home. At the same precise time the camera crew watching Jaytee observed and filmed the little dog making his way to the window, apparently knowing somehow that Smart would soon be there.

So you think you know how Jaytee did it – right? I bet you think that the smart little dog had learned the distinctive sound that Smart's car made and with keen doggy hearing could pick up its impending arrival long before the ears of the investigators and camera crew.

A good theory, but it doesn't explain the fact that Dr. Sheldrake had

Smart come home in a taxi cab, just to prevent such a possibility!

Another investigator involved in the testing of Jaytee, Dr. Heinz Leger, threw what he thought would be yet another wrench into the works.

"We also tried to fool the dog at one point by telling Miss Smart we wanted her to go to her sister's home, but the dog did not respond. Only when we gave the instruction to return home did the dog go to the window and stay there," Dr. Leger ruefully admitted.

Jaytee's amazing ability is being put to further tests. On one occasion, Smart had to return home from an incredible distance of 50 miles. As her car entered her hometown of Blackpool, Jaytee headed for the window. Lloyd Auerbach, director of the San Francisco-based Office of Paranormal Investigation, says dogs have extremely heightened powers of ESP for two very good reasons:

"One is because they love us and emotional ties seem to amplify psychic ability," the well-known researcher says. "Secondly, no one has ever told dogs that being psychic is weird. Dogs and other animals are not restricted by someone in their culture telling them they can't do this," he adds.

A most chilling "tail" ...

Still one more story from writer Bill Shull's collection sends real chills down the spine. He tells it in these words:

"Robin Deland was driving on an unpaved, narrow and winding road near Gunnison, Colorado, one night, when suddenly a dog appeared in his headlights. Deland braked to a stop and sat frozen in his seat. The dog was Jeff – his collie that had died six months ago!

"Jeff leaped from the car and called out the name of his beloved dog, but Jeff spun and ran off," Shull continues.

Determined to get to the bottom of the eerie mystery, Deland followed but could not catch up to the dog he was absolutely convinced had been his. What he found instead was a place in the road where a piece of the highway had given way. Had he not been stopped by the ghost of Jeff, Deland and his car would have plunged to a horrifying death.

If only they had listened...

The following are stories about people who should have listened to their dogs. If they had, the stories would have had happier endings.

Dr. Ute Pleimes of the University of Giessen, West Germany, has for years collected and investigated instances of ESP in animals. She gives this example of a woman who ignored her dog's warning, when it might have saved her life.

The woman had borrowed a neighbor's car. The neighbor's dog did everything in his limited power to stop her from driving away. The dog growled angrily and tried to snatch the keys from her hand.

The woman had a hard time shaking the dog off. As she drove away, the dog followed, yelping, until he could no longer keep up. An hour later, the car skidded and hit a wall. The woman was killed instantly.

The *Watford Evening Echo* published a story in 1971 about a five-year-old collie named Laddie who accompanied his master every day since puppyhood to the slate quarry where the owner worked.

This had been the dog's routine for years, but one morning, he refused to leave the house. Nothing would persuade him to move, and for the first time his master, Robert Hayes, went to work alone.

Just before noon, there was an explosion at the quarry. Hayes was killed.

Here's a happy ending...

This owner listened to his dog – and lived to tell about it:

Josef Becker went for a walk with his Alsatian named Strulli one day and stopped at a local bar. The dog suddenly became agitated, doing everything possible to attract attention, running around in circles, howling at his master, tugging at his clothes and trying to drag him from his seat.

Strulli was such a nuisance that Becker, intent on finishing his drink, put the dog outside and shut the door.

Somehow the dog got back inside and again began to tug frantically at Becker's clothing. Tired of this losing battle and seeing that he would never be able to finish his drink in peace, Becker left the bar at two minutes before five. Two minutes later, to the deafening crash of timber, bricks and plaster, the building collapsed on its occupants, killing nine people and injuring more than 20 others.

OH, HOW SMART THEY ARE

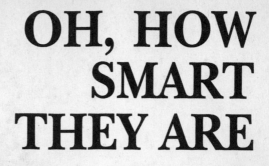

If you pick up a starving dog and make him prosperous, he will not bite you. This is the principal difference between a dog and a man.

Mark Twain

Have we learned more from our dogs than we think?

It is all well and good for us to act smug about teaching old dogs – or young ones – new tricks, but it would be downright ungrateful of us not to acknowledge that dogs have taught us a thing or two.

Just in case you know someone who thinks of Rover merely as a gerbil that barks, you'll want to make them aware of yet one more important role our canine companions have played down through the ages that they have been our friends: their wonderful symbolism as teachers of life's important lessons.

49

For almost as long as humankind has been thinking about and writing down possible answers to the eternal questions we've pondered and wondered about, the inspiration for thousands of useful observations has been our friend, the dog.

On the ancient streets of Greece and Rome, ordinary folks found wonderful little truths and bits of wisdom that they shared with one another after observing the habits, character, friendliness and helpfulness of dogs.

Using their four-pawed friends to illustrate a point, humans put what they learned into short, meaning-packed and often humorous sayings that served as the last word in many an argument.

Historians, linguists and folklorists call those profound little insights proverbs.

The proverbs our ancestors wrote were often small sermons, meant to be passed along as much more important ideas, advice and warnings that anyone could understand.

Many of those quaint sayings are still in our vocabularies today. Certainly we all know it is best to *"let sleeping dogs lie."* Then there are the times when we're unhappy to learn that something we have done has put us *"in the doghouse."*

"Leading a dog's life" seems a trifle quaint to us today – at least here in the United States, where dogs lead a pretty good life for the most part. But in days of old it wasn't all Kibbles and Bits®, and the life of many a dog was not so good. Those examples are only a few among hundreds which scholars and street urchins alike could draw on to express themselves clearly about dozens of topics.

"A lean dog will get through hedges," one old proverb said. This means that a thin person had a better chance of recovering from an illness than a person grossly overweight.

A pretty savvy medical observation, considering the era in which it was coined.

When gossiping about a tightwad, our ancestors would often say: *"He would not give his bone to a dog."* A harsh statement that needs no further explanation.

And speaking of gossip: *"A dog that fetches will carry"* the citizens of Rome would say, meaning that if someone was willing to tell you secrets about another, they would just as likely tell your secrets, too!

A wealthy man of the Middle Ages drew chuckled when, after buying an expensive guard dog at a rural fair, he was seen to throw away the key to his house:

"I will not keep a dog and bark myself," he explained.

The legendary St. Bernard (the man, not the dog) is credited with coming up with the statement *"love me, love my dog."* When he said it in the 12th century, those who heard him knew he wasn't just talking about the lovable big beast that would one day bear his name, but knew he was offering a star to steer by that applied to many aspects of everyday life. If you'd like to show off some time, you may quote St. Bernard in the original Latin by saying: *"Que me amat, amat et canem meum."* Let them figure that one out!

A large heaping of scorn and shame was packed into this proverb aimed at scoundrels and cowards: *"He that strikes my dog would strike me, if he dared!"*

Our forebears knew of the extra courage that flowed through their veins when they fought to save their own land when the scourge of war arose. They credited the dog with the same sense of courage: *"Every dog is valiant at his own house,"* they said. Some knew there was a deeper meaning that could be read into that double-edged observation.

Because they admired the determination of the canine once he had taken on a task, the words *"dogged determination"* became a part of our descriptive language.

That same persistence was praised in still another proverb: *"The hindmost dog may yet catch the hare."* That motivational spur was spoken to boys of the time to urge them not to give up too easily in the face of a difficult task.

To call a person an *"old dog"* was no insult to our ancestors. This meant that one being so described had been around and knew what was what.

A curious expression that reaches back to the times of the Pharaohs in ancient Egypt preached a warning on the foolishness of drinking too much or too recklessly.

"Drink like a dog at the Nile," that old warning cautioned. This warning seems baffling at first glance. What it alluded to was the fact that huge crocodiles on the banks of the Nile River always laid in wait for the dogs who came there for a cool sip of water in the hopes of snapping their huge jaws shut on one who would serve as their dinner.

The dogs who drank at the banks of the Nile learned to be wary, sipped their drinks in moderation and left before trouble could strike. Good advice then – and now.

The proverbial dog was misused from time to time to illustrate an undesirable human trait:

To be a *"dog in a manger"* was to be a person so low as to deny another person something for which you personally had no need. This proverb comes from a fable by Aesop in which a bad-tempered dog climbed into the hay manger and barked so ferociously when the oxen came to eat that the oxen were kept away from their dinner – even though the ill-tempered dog had no real use of the hay.

"There is a dog in the well," our ancestors would say when they harbored a suspicion that something was wrong, even though they had yet to figure out just what that something was.

"Dogs bark as they are bred" was a none-too-subtle proverb put-down back in olden times. This saying still punctures the balloon of the clumsy social climber of today.

"She's everyone's dog that whistles" was a proverb first said by lustful sailors of the middle ages. I don't think this requires much elaboration.

Taking a *"hair of the dog that bit you"* was an actual remedy tried by dog-bite victims of Julius Caesar's times on the optimistic notion that like poison would cancel out a like. Today we put that proverb to work in a more civilized way. Bloody Mary, anyone?

If you worked hard, prayed, minded your own business and you were a good friend, then before death claimed you the world would take note, so our early relatives believed. They spoke of that certainty in this charming way: *"Every man will have his hour; every dog will have his day."*

A FRIEND TILL THE END

Dogs lives are too short...
their only fault, really.
Agnes Sligh Turnbull

We love our dogs for many reasons, but surely one of the most beautiful things in the world is the love – and the loyalty – they return so generously to us.

No other animal has proven so many countless times and in so many extraordinary ways how deep is the bond of affection between us.

The stories of the loyalty of dogs to master and mistress run as a wonderful and golden thread throughout history and it is worth telling several here.

Bobby – His loyalty never died...

There is one particularly loyal dog that stands apart from all the rest. This is the story of an incredible dog who remained faithful to his master even in death. All of Europe had heard about this dog in the mid-1800s.

His name was Bobby. He was a shivering, cold Skye terrier that was found on the streets of Edinburgh, Scotland, and adopted by a softhearted police constable by the name of Jock Gray.

In the years that followed the pair were inseparable. Bobby followed Officer Gray on his rounds each day. At noon they took their lunch together at Ramsay's Inn where Gray dined on the blue plate special and Bobby was always given a bun dipped in the tasty sauces from his master's plate.

Friends of the familiar pair were saddened when Jock Gray died unexpectedly in 1858, but no one mourned the dead policeman more than his devoted pal Bobby.

Bobby attended Officer Gray's funeral, but would not leave the grave site after the service, despite the coaxing of many friends who would have taken him in and given the grieving pooch a new home.

When the forlorn friend showed up at Ramsay's Inn precisely at noon the day following Gray's funeral, kindhearted friends slipped the dog his usual tasty bun, then watched in surprise as Bobby scampered off with his lunch, heading in the direction of the quiet churchyard cemetery where his master now rested.

Some who followed Bobby were touched to see the loyal dog lay down by Gray's grave before nibbling at the morsel he'd been given – Bobby was having lunch with Gray again!

More amazing still was that Bobby repeated that

touching demonstration each day without fail for the next nine years. He left Gray's grave only for those few minutes that it took to make the trip to the cafe and then returned to stay by Gray's grave again.

A few years later, the city fathers of Edinburgh passed a law that all dogs must be licensed. When the question of Bobby's ownership arose, it wasn't really much of a question at all.

By a special resolution, the city adopted the loyal little terrier. They gave him the name "Greyfriar's Bobby" and ordered a special collar and tag made for him. The city stated that his annual license fee was forever paid for due to his loving devotion to the master whose side he would not leave – even in death.

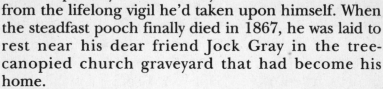

Advancing age, weakened legs and dimming eyes did not keep Greyfriar's Bobby from the lifelong vigil he'd taken upon himself. When the steadfast pooch finally died in 1867, he was laid to rest near his dear friend Jock Gray in the tree-canopied church graveyard that had become his home.

Some have claimed to see the ghosts of Gray and Bobby making their rounds late at night on the foggy streets of Edinburgh. If ever there were ghosts one wished to believe in, surely it is the kindhearted cop and the dog who loved him.

Jim – The most amazing dog that ever was...

Millions of Americans were saddened when they picked up their newspapers in mid-March of 1937 and learned of the death of an amazing dog the whole nation had talked about, puzzled over and taken to their hearts – a black and white setter who was given a name that told some – but not all – of his incredible story. His master had named him "Jim." The media would soon change it to "Jim the Wonderdog."

To this day, the unbelievable skills that Jim demonstrated before astonished witnesses are still not fully understood, even though they were thoroughly investigated with every tool that science had at the time. What was so special about Jim?

How astonished would you be to find that your pet could not only understand every word you said, and into the bargain, read your mind and the minds of others – but could even understand you when they were thinking or speaking in a foreign language?

Those were just a few of the surprises Jim sprung on his startled owner, Sam Van Arsdale, a small-town Missouri businessman who got his first inkling of his pet's uncanny powers while taking a quiet stroll in the woods on a warm spring morning.

With Jim trotting at his side, Van Arsdale mentally picked out a hickory tree up ahead as a place where he planned to stop and rest for a few minutes beneath its inviting shade.

Without thinking about it, he spoke aloud: "That hickory tree looks like a good place to rest for a while," he said.

Jim suddenly broke into a run, heading for the exact hickory tree that Van Arsdale had chosen. The dog then sat there grinning and wagging his tail as a baffled Van Arsdale caught up, wondering to himself how Jim had known which tree he had been talking about.

Curious about what he was certain was a strange coincidence, Sam told Jim that maybe an oak tree would be more to his liking as a resting spot.

Seconds later, Jim took off and waited for his shocked master beneath the leafy boughs of a giant oak.

Van Arsdale then named off several other kinds of trees he knew were nearby. "Walnut, elm, sycamore..." Van Arsdale said in turn. Each time, Jim rushed straight over to the kind of tree his master had just named.

In the months that followed, Jim's ability to understand English exploded to the utter amazement of Van Arsdale's family and everyone in the small town who could not solve the riddle of the clever "tricks" they were sure Sam was secretly teaching the dog.

Jim's fame spread like a prairie fire and a reluctant Van Arsdale quickly found himself "hounded" to bring the amazing pooch to local county fairs and church socials to entertain curious country folks.

A newspaper reported on one such demonstration that Jim performed for the residents of Warsaw, Missouri:

"When his master, Sam Van Arsdale, asked Jim to identify the town doctor, Jim trotted right over to Dr. Savage and nudged him," the stunned reporter who covered the event wrote.

"When he was asked to find a car with the license number 132875, Jim went over and placed his paws on the running board of the car with that very license number."

Jim next did something even more amazing, the newspaper said:

"Then when he was asked – this time in French – to find a Bible in the crowd, he walked over to the Methodist minister and nudged his pocket. There was a Bible inside."

Before long, Jim attracted the attention of the State Legislature of Missouri who wanted to see for themselves the dog that had rapidly become the most famous citizen of their state.

True to form, Jim the Wonderdog stunned the assembled lawmakers when he carried out commands given to him in shorthand – and then in Morse code.

When he was told by those two methods to go to the desk of selected members of the senate and the house, Jim trotted over to the person named and extended a friendly paw for them to shake.

Scientists at the University of Missouri said they wouldn't be so easily taken in. They demanded that Van Arsdale allow them to run a series of controlled tests on Jim.

The smiling dog passed every test that those hard-nosed researchers created. Asked in German to find a girl wearing a blue dress, Jim went quickly through a crowd and found one. Ordered in Spanish to find a man with a mustache, Jim did just that.

The tests that Jim was given were filmed, and researchers today still cannot offer any explanation for the dog's amazing skills than doctors of years ago. They concluded that no trickery was involved. Jim simply seemed to possess some kind of understanding they could not understand.

Even though Jim had already proven to be the world's most amazing dog, he later developed ANOTHER utterly unexplainable power. Jim was able to predict future events!

For seven years in a row, the pooch was shown slips of paper containing the names of the horses that would run in the famous Kentucky Derby. After studying them, Jim would firmly place his paw on one. For seven straight years, the wonder dog accurately predicted which horse would win the race.

When a famous magazine of the era predicted the defeat of presidential candidate Franklin Roosevelt by his opponent Alf Landon, Jim "said" otherwise. He was right again.

Jim's eerie powers of prediction caused dozens of offers to roll in from people wanting to buy him for huge amounts of cash. Van Arsdale said Jim wasn't for sale – at any price – and once turned down a bid of $250,000!

As Jim grew older, Van Arsdale became more and more concerned about the health of his incredible friend and feared that all the appearances were wearing the great dog down. Van Arsdale decided it was time for Jim to retire and they both did so in the little village of Marshall.

It was here that Jim slipped peacefully away one night at age 12, leaving behind him millions whom he had caused to take a new and long look at their own pets and wonder what unknown things lay behind their friendly, but sometimes mysterious faces.

Arlecchino – The canine secretary...

Jim was not the only dog in history who performed amazing feats – there have been others who've exhibited some skills for which science has no rational explanation.

To briefly mention another, there is the case of Arlecchino – curiously enough also a setter – and the special pet of Italian animal trainer Elizabeth Borghese.

When still a young pup, Arlecchino developed the habit of crashing his big paws on the keyboard of Elizabeth's typewriter, seeming to enjoy the clatter it made.

Amused, Elizabeth wondered if Arlecchino could actually learn to type, and after months of patient experimenting it turned out that the pup was a virtual John "Steinbark," learning to tap out with his nose a vocabulary of more than 20 words.

On one occasion, it appeared to astonished observers that Arlecchino wasn't just turning out random doggy drivel, but doing some real reasoning. Asked the question "What do you like to do?" the talented animal paused for a moment, then pecked out the word "car" on the typewriter keys, describing the thing he liked most in the world to do – go for a ride in his owner's car.

Dorsey –
Postman of the
Wild West...

Another unusual pooch is believed to be the only dog who ever officially worked for the U.S. Post Office. His name was Dorsey and the years were 1883 to 1886. The place: The wild and wooly mining areas of California where postmaster Jim Stacy carried the mail between remote camps scattered near Calico and Bismarck.

His constant companion on the lonely treks was the mix-breed shepherd he'd found left behind when a once-lively camp became a ghost town. Stacy gave his new pet the name Dorsey in honor of a friend back east. When Stacy suddenly became ill, mail backed up in his small office and desperate miners complained that needed items were not reaching them.

Stacy wondered if Dorsey remembered the route well enough to make the rounds himself, equipped with saddlebag pouches that fit over the sturdy dog's big shoulders.

Sure enough, Dorsey did, and for months the hard-working canine delivered the U.S. mail and was treated to steak dinners and an occasional slurp or two of beer by the grateful miners for whom the mail came through in a most unusual way.

A special tag made up in Washington proclaimed Dorsey an official employee of the postal service. A letter of commendation from the Postmaster General and Dorsey's well-worn leather saddlebags hung on the walls of the small post office for many years.

Ariel – The Fireman's Friend...

For every dog that captures our attention in some dramatic way, there are thousands more who do things that add to the quality of many lives without coming so prominently to the public's notice. Consider, as a nice example, a bright-eyed Dalmatian named Ariel, the pride of the neighborhood fire station in Merriam, Kansas.

Ariel is the buddy of the brave smoke-eaters who serve the station, but she's also a great teacher. Local firefighters take her around to area schools to acquaint kids with fire safety tips that could save their lives.

The patient firefighters have taught Ariel the "stop, drop and roll" maneuver they want kids to learn just in case they should be the victim of a clothing fire.

Imagine the impact on the youngsters and how long they'll remember a lifesaving safety procedure taught to them by a tail-wagging friend who gets to live with real firefighters and ride on those shiny red trucks!

Chexx, Callie and Silki –
"This won't hurt a bit!"

And then there are the three patient little Maltese dogs that pediatric dentist Neale Eckstein uses in his practice with kids to help them overcome the fear of going to the dentist.

Chexx, Callie and Silki got their job by accident when Dr. Eckstein brought them to his office one day so they wouldn't be lonely. The kids who encountered them had a ball and Dr. Eckstein noticed something else – the children were having such a good time that they forgot to be afraid!

Now the tail-wagging trio are a permanent part of his "staff" and kids can't wait to come for their next checkup.

With rigorous hygiene observed, the dentist allows the children to hold one of the pets while they sit in his chair and he performs whatever work is required.

"The dogs disarm even the most apprehensive patients," Dr. Eckstein told the editor of the newsletter *Your Dog*.

Mirko – A sick child's
best friend...

One of the most touching stories you will ever hear about dog heroes is that of a family of world champion Rottweilers owned by a Texas family who decided to share their magnificent animals with those who desperately needed love.

It is the story of Richard and Vee Wayland, husband

65

and wife, and Mirko, J.R., Anvil and Candy, their incredible dogs.

It was Vee Wayland who showed Mirko in international dog shows where he became the top Rottweiler champ of his breed. Then, as the champion aged, his owner came across an article about the use of dogs in therapy for persons with life-threatening illnesses.

Mirko had to win new kinds of competitions before a local children's hospital was satisfied the dog could safely become a regular visitor to their critical care wards. As in every other competition, the big, friendly, 125-pound bundle of affection passed those tests with flying colors.

Before long, Mirko was performing miracles and the staff wondered how they had ever managed without the gentle giant who had become the most effective therapist they'd ever seen. Within a few months, Mirko was a welcome visitor on every floor of the hospital. The miracles continued:

In an article written for a medical magazine by Richard Wayburn, he told one of those stories in these words:

"One of the most unforgettable patients was an eight-year-old boy suffering from cancer. He was violently ill from chemotherapy and had just been told by his doctors that he was losing his sight. He cried for hours. As Mirko neared his bed, the little boy threw his arms around the dog's neck and whispered to Mirko that he was going to be blind.

"The dog allowed this helpless little victim to finally verbalize his innermost fears and eventually face them," Wayburn recalled.

J.R. – A beautiful
tradition continues...

Within months, the selfless husband and wife had trained one of Mirko's sons – J.R. – to take over where his father had left off. Before long, J.R. had eased the terrible sense of loss that staff and patients alike had felt at Mirko's passing. Wayburn tells how J.R. has been doing:

"Recently I accompanied Vee and J.R. on their rounds at an intensive care rehabilitation center. I watched as J.R. gave a 'high five' to a 49-year-old man who had suffered a severe stroke and can't talk, but is learning to use a spelling board. When asked who his favorite person was, the stroke patient pointed an unsteady finger to a 'J' and an 'R.'"

And J.R. is not alone in carrying on the incredible work of Mirko. Another two of his offspring, Anvil and Candy, have been trained to do the same healing tasks.

Another sibling, named Promise, has become the companion to a young Missouri mother who suffers from multiple sclerosis. One night a fire broke out in her home. Promise awakened his mistress and led her to safety. Mirko, looking on from his special place in Heaven, must have been very proud.

He wrote of another of the dog's gifts to a human friend:

"A retired veterinarian had suffered a mild stroke. He then learned that he also had cancer and went into total depression. He had not gotten out of bed nor spoken to his wife or daughter for days. But when Mirko visited, he got out of bed, hugged the dog and asked that his picture be taken with Mirko. Then he began talking to his family.

"Later, the man's wife thanked Vee, with tears in her eyes," Wayburn wrote.

In some rooms, the condition of a patient was such that Mirko wasn't allowed to enter. The great dog learned to sit in the doorway and wave a paw of cheer and good wishes to the patient. Into other rooms he carried little baskets of gifts, a get-well card, a bookmark, a small toy, a little sign that read "I love you."

For more than two years Mirko made his remarkable rounds and then, in an ironic twist of fate, developed a form of canine cancer that took his wonderful life. Wayburn described a small part of the dog's legacy:

"How much Mirko was missed was demonstrated by a man named Roosevelt. Roosevelt was a stroke victim who had limited use of his limbs and hadn't been able to utter a word for months.

"The staff hadn't had the heart to tell him Mirko had died. However, after three weeks of no visits from Mirko, the nurses were astounded when, with tremendous effort, Roosevelt uttered an anxious one-word question:

'Dog?'"

LET'S TALK ABOUT DOGS

Blessed is the person who has earned
the love of an old dog.

Sidney Jeanne Seward

What people are saying:

We talk *to* our dogs, and *about* our dogs, too. It appears that almost every dog owner down through history has had something to say about their special pet – or dogs in general.

Celebrated American writer Mark Twain pointed out this razor-edged truth:

> "If you pick up a starving dog and make him prosperous, he will not bite you. This is the principal difference between a dog and a man."

Novelist and essayist Edward Hoagland did not have his tongue too far in his cheek when he offered this advice:

> 🦴 "In order to really enjoy a dog, one doesn't merely try to train him to be semi-human. The point of it is to open oneself to the possibility of becoming partly a dog."

And of the warm understanding the canine has for us, famed English author Samuel Butler remarked:

> 🦴 "The great pleasure of a dog is that you may make a fool of yourself with him and not only will he not scold you, but he will make a fool of himself, too."

A dog's love of playing and his patience with kids was celebrated by Henry Ward Beecher when he noted:

> 🦴 "The dog was created especially for children. He is the god of frolic."

Humorist Fran Liebowitz had this advice for dogs in a book she wrote:

> 🦴 "If your master wants you to wear a sweater, ask him to wag his tail."

The scary stuff which legends are made of ...

Perhaps because dogs are so open and friendly – not mysterious and standoffish like the cat tends to be – we were not as quick to link them to our darkest superstitions, dreams and fears.

Unlike the cat – who never deserved the unfair rap

she got, I must say – dogs, with some exceptions, don't have to carry around with them the baggage of such an unkind past.

However, there were parts of the world where the dog found himself associated with many mischievous legends.

The proud Vikings assigned a huge, fierce black hound to Odin – their principal god – as his loyal companion. The Vikings who raided and terrorized the coast of early Britain often had trained attack dogs as part of their invading force.

The terror of those raids may have given rise to the superstition that a fearsome devil-dog named Black Shuck has haunted those parts of Britain for hundreds of centuries and remains an occasional menace to this very day.

Black Shuck is said by those who have claimed to see him to be jet-black and huge – the size of a calf – with fiercely glowing red eyes the size of saucers. His feet make no sound and he leaves no tracks and has been seen most often in old church burial grounds.

Some believers, walking lonely roads at night, say they have felt Black Shuck's icy breath on their necks and fled in terror, casting a backward glance, only to find still more horror – a headless Black Shuck.

In some areas of ancient Scotland, a New Year's custom turned the family dog into a temporary scapegoat. In that superstitious ritual, the dog was first given a piece of sweetbread, and then shooed out the front door by the woman of the house as she recited these words:

"Whatever death of men, or loss of cattle, would

happen in this house to the end of the present year, may it all light on your head."

The bewildered dog was allowed to return to the fireside within a few hours, apparently no worse for the wear, probably wagging a tail and grinning to see if there was another crumb or two of that tasty dish left.

The howling of dogs was taken to be a bad omen in many cultures. Some cultures actually believe that the barking of dogs can foretell the death of someone in the family. An encyclopedia of country wisdom from the year 1651 had this to say about howling dogs:

"That dogs with their howling forecast death ... is plain by history and experience," that book warned. The diary of writer Henry Cullwick, penned in 1863, illustrated how deeply that belief put down its roots:

"I got a letter to say my Aunt Ellen was dead. I quite expected it, for the dog came in yesterday morning and howled piteously," the writer wrote with certainty.

Dogs and the law...

The usual way in which dogs and the law collide is through the nipping of a mailman or a breach of some local ordinance regarding leashes or license tags. However, they have, on occasion, been the center of some big-time legal issues.

Imagine how pleased the nearly 150 stray dogs who had been adopted by oil heiress Eleanor Richey were when they "heard" that they were the beneficiaries of her $4.3 million estate when her will was probated in a Florida court in 1968.

The kindly old lady left specific details about how her beloved little family were to be cared for. Her requests were carried out for more than 15 years, until the last of her heirs died of old age.

The dogs had lived in comfortable surroundings on the 180-acre ranch where she had collected and cared for them while she was still alive.

Those who complained that Richey's fortune had "gone to the dogs," didn't take into account the shrewdness of this good-hearted animal lover.

All of the money she left behind for the care of her adoptees was invested in a trust that not only earned enough to see to the dogs' continued future happiness, but actually made a profit to boot.

When the last pooch, named Musketeer, went on to his reward, the trust, which had grown to a whopping $12 million, was given to another cause that Richey had wanted to aid.

Animal scientists at Auburn University School of Veterinary Medicine have since put those millions to good use to go on helping the creatures Richey had loved so much.

However, not all legacies intended to benefit dogs have turned out as well as that of Richey's...

Asleep on the job...

In a recent book *Death and Beyond*, lawyers Gerald Green and Jeffrey Condon tell the tale of an elderly lady named Mrs. Green (no relation to the author) who made a provision in her will that Chauncey, her black Labrador, continue to live in her home, watched over by a guardian who was to be paid a salary of $1,000 a month and who would live rent-free as Chauncey's caretaker.

A trust officer of the bank was supposed to oversee the arrangements.

What Mrs. Green hadn't anticipated was that even bankers go to heaven sometimes – as did the trust officer.

In the shuffle of papers and the transfer of duties that followed, junior members of the bank staff were given the task of making the required regular visits to the house where Chauncey lived to make certain that all the provisions of Mrs. Green's will were being carried out.

The duty of checking up on a dog was hardly considered a prize job at the bank. Those stuck with the task quickly passed on the responsibility as they climbed the corporate ladder.

It was not until some 12 years after Mrs. Green's death that anyone stopped to do what should have been a fairly obvious calculation:

Chauncey was nine when his mistress died. To have survived 12 more years would have made him 21 years old – quite a rare and unusual age for a dog.

It finally dawned on the bank's trust department that something might be amiss. A further investigation then showed that Chauncey had gone to his own reward five years after Mrs. Green had died.

He had been replaced – not once, but twice, with new look-alike black Labs so that the greedy caretaker could continue living his cushy rent-free and comfortably salaried life.

Stamps of approval...

No animal has been more frequently given the honor of appearing on postage stamps than man's best friend. Experts on stamp collecting say it would be almost impossible to count how many millions of stamps bearing pictures of the dog have been issued by the nations of the world just in this century.

A writer for *Stamp Magazine* – the stamp collector's Bible – says that many dog lovers who don't even think of themselves as stamp collectors have nonetheless purchased and saved many of the beautiful and colorful stamps issued in honor of the dog.

This same writer recommends such a collection as a wonderful way to make our children aware of the importance of their pet.

While the U.S. Postal Service through the years has produced numerous canine issues, one of the most interesting was a 1994 stamp celebrating the Chinese new year – which in that Oriental zodiac marked 1994 as the year of the dog.

A country that consistently prints handsome dog stamps is the little nation of Monaco – the country that dog lover Princess Grace helped rule until her tragic death. Since 1970, Monaco has offered stamp collectors and dog lovers a new series of stamps each year, each featuring a different dog breed.

Some collectors save stamps honoring their favorite kind of dog. Virtually every breed has had its day.

Stamps also have been created to celebrate the anniversary of major animal protection groups, such as Britain's pioneer Royal Society for the Prevention of Cruelty Toward Animals.

The German shepherd has been saluted many times on the face of stamps issued by Germany, but other countries have also honored this highly popular breed – Afghanistan, Czechoslovakia, Guinea, Laos and tiny Dhomey.

America joined in the tribute by issuing a stamp that portrayed the shepherd in one of his many useful roles, that of guide dog for the blind.

The works of famous artists, such as Britain's George Stubbs, who painted both royal and common dogs in the 18th century, have been reproduced as stamps.

A commemorative set of that artist's work offered by that country's postal service is considered by collectors to be one of the most striking ever produced – a set of five that went on sale in 1991 sold out almost at once.

The German postal service, which turns out numerous stamps featuring dogs, issued one batch that had a much more useful purpose than just delivering the mail.

Called the *Fur die Jugend* – For the Children – series, the proceeds from the sale of those stamps went to projects that helped the nation's youths.

Another prized set of stamps included a famous dog and human heroes. The nation of Guyana paid tribute to space pioneers John Glenn, Neil Armstrong and Youri Gagarine with stamps it produced in 1994. Proudly displayed next to those valiant voyagers was the Russian dog Laika, whom the Soviet Union sent into space in 1957.

Protecting our innocent friends...

There have been times in our long-standing relationship with the canine that they have been cruelly used and abused by ignorant and evil people. But, thank goodness, more loving and enlightened friends had the courage to step forward to protect them.

The riff-raff of Europe in the 17th century found a particularly perverse pleasure in the "sport" of bull-baiting. A large bull was tied firmly to the ground and torn to its death by dogs bred and trained to be their opponents in the bloody ring.

The Europeans had not invented this barbaric game. History reports that the ancient Romans first made it a part of the savage gladiator contests in the Coliseum. They brought it with them when they conquered other parts of the world. It reached its sad height of popularity in Britain in the early 1600s.

Originally, any dog that could be encouraged to enter the brawl would do. But as the cruel sport took hold, heartless trainers perfected the breed that came to be known as the English bulldog. This breed proved to be the deadliest champion in the bull-baiting arena.

Old English mastiffs and feisty terriers were mated to produce the squat-standing, huge-jawed and ferocious fighters that proved to be almost immune to the terrible pain of the wounds they suffered when the enraged bull defended itself.

It was not until 1822 that public outrage put an end to bull-baiting in England with the passage by Parliament of what was called "The Ill Treatment of Cattle Bill." However, it made no provision for animals kept as pets.

Humane societies...

A movement to put into law basic rights for other animals – including dogs – was started by the Royal Society for the Prevention of Cruelty Toward Animals (RSPCA) in the 1840s.

This group became the model for a similar organization that is familiar to us all today – the American Society for the Prevention of Cruelty Toward Animals (ASPCA), which was founded in New York City in 1866 by Henry Berg. It was the inspiration for hundreds of local and national humane societies and non-profit groups who look out for our friends to this day.

Civilized people who admired the raw courage of the bulldog – but not the terrible activities which they had been forced to participate in – took it upon themselves to begin re-breeding the line. The result is the scary-looking, but actually quite gentle bulldog we now know and love today.

The scrappy bulldog's legendary courage however, has survived as a symbol of bravery and dedication. He is the official mascot of the United States Marine Corps.

Yet another heartless sport that was a favorite among the peasants of France throughout the Middle Ages was the pitting of dog against dog in a fight to the death on which the spectators would bet upon their favorite.

In those horrible contests, a huge French mastiff that came to be called the *Dogue de Bordeaux* emerged as the most popular breed of fighting dog.

History remembers one especially brutal exhibition that took place at a nobleman's estate: A wild jaguar was introduced into the dog fight to create an even more ghastly, more brutal, even bloodier show.

As in Britain, the outrage against such sick and barbaric entertainment finally grew strong enough for the passage of laws that put an end to it.

(In World War I, when Frenchmen looked skyward and saw the fierce duels between the German and Allied flyers, the word that sprang to their mind was "dogfight." It then became a part of our language.)

It's (not) a dog's life

In these modern times, our dogs enjoy much better than a "dog's life" in most parts of the world. However, there are still places where all is not Milkbone® Biscuits and steak bones.

In China, where an often overwhelmed government struggles to feed its hungry masses, bureaucrats calculated that the dog population of that sprawling nation had gotten out of hand.

They estimated that the dogs of the country consumed each day enough food to feed 40 million people. That statistic prompted the government to place a staggering tax on Chinese dog owners that was – for many people – the equivalent of a year's wages.

(Continued on page 81)

The bureaucrats also passed stiff regulations and laws that forbid those living in certain overpopulated cities ownership of any dog taller than 13 inches or longer than 25 inches. Many dog owners have taken to hiding their pets because they can't afford the outrageous tag fee. The country's emerging yuppie class have been paying prices as high as $10,000 for tiny imported dogs such as Chihuahuas and Pomeranians, according to New China News Agency reports.

The current Chinese government's harsh attitude toward the canine is in sharp contrast to the way their ancient ancestors have loved and respected the dog since the beginning of civilization.

In Chinese astrology, one of the most important celestial benefactors is the dog. In a country where there are countless rituals associated with the bringing on of good luck, one of the most enduring is the belief that great fortune will befall you if a stray dog enters the courtyard or front door of your home.

Can dogs see in color?

The noble and trusty seeing-eye dog that the visually impaired have come to rely upon as their own eyes is a wonderful choice for a friend who can safely lead them. However – truth be told – canine vision is far from the keenest in the animal kingdom.

But there's no need to worry. The tremendously sharp senses of smell and hearing combine to compensate to the visual shortcomings of of friend the dog.

While the canine eye is constructed much like the human eye, Fido's view of what goes on around him is different than ours in some very important ways.

First, dogs see the world for the most part in shades of gray. Their color vision mechanism does allow them to see limited shades of red and blue, but yellow, green and orange are pretty much lost to them.

Our eyes are capable of clearly seeing a brown rabbit standing in front of a green bush wiggling its ears. But the canine eye would first be drawn to the bunny's whereabouts by scent and then by the frightened sounds the rabbit makes after it has been discovered.

Only then would the dog begin focusing in. His eyes, unlike ours, are capable of receiving independent information from either eye that can hone in on motion across a very wide field.

As Mother Nature decided what needed to be in our pet's optical package, color was considered excess baggage. What color the rabbit was didn't matter as long as the dog could sense it, locate it and chase it!

While dogs can see far distances very well – much better than we can – their vision close up is not as good as ours, and diminishes further with age. Things at hand seem slightly blurry. If dogs took to reading the morning paper, they would surely need glasses.

A dog's night vision is far superior to ours. Because they were hunters originally, they come equipped with a built-in light-gathering mechanism that permits them to see in much lower light than we humans.

The keenness of your pet's vision varies from breed to breed. Short nosed dogs such as the Bulldog have eyes that are placed differently than a long-nosed dog such as a collie. This gives each breed of dog a slightly different view of the world – in some ways better, in others ways, more limited.

OUR PAMPERED POOCHES

A dog is not "almost human" and I know of no greater insult to the canine race than to describe it as such. The dog can do many things which man cannot do, never could do and never will.

John Holmes

There is no exact figure of the amount of money we spend on toys and special treats for our dogs or the money we cheerfully spend at the vet to make certain that our favorite pets live a long, happy and healthy life. The best estimates calculate the amount is almost $20 billion each year.

Across America, countless jobs exist solely for the purpose of creating both ordinary and exotic pooch products. Some very imaginative businesses thrive on the special love we have for our four-footed friends and our desire to pamper them in unusual – and sometimes expensive – ways.

Eat up!

In Kansas City, Missouri, favored Fidos have their own dog bakery. Called the Three Dog Bakery, owners Mark Beckloff and Dan Dye pull from their ovens every day more than 50 varieties of treats formulated especially to tickle a pooch's palate.

Some pups prefer a little biscuit called "Collie Flower" while others bark for St. Bernard Bars or Scotty-Biscottis.

All are prepared from totally natural ingredients such as veggies and yogurt, coconut, peanuts and homemade beef stew. All of the recipes are approved by veterinarians and have been taste-tested by Beckloff's and Dye's dogs before going on sale.

And if you think a bakery turning out treats for dogs isn't the greatest moneymaker you could imagine – guess again! In less than five years, the pair have opened four more stores and have watched their bow-wow business go past the million-dollar mark in sales every year.

Not only do customers flock through the doors of Three Dog Bakery, the company now does a thriving mail-order business, filling more than 25,000 customer requests each year. Among the dogs who wait for the mailman to deliver the latest batch of Collie Flowers are Oprah Winfrey's dogs.

Only in Hollywood – (then again, maybe not!)

Not to be outdone in the slightest are the trendy dogs of Tinseltown who have their own favorite boutique called Critter Caterers of Beverly Hills. This store not only offers chic cuisine, but a host of other things no Hollywood dog can do without.

On the menu of this store operated by Tracy Parsons is beef- or chicken-flavored bottled water and a specially concocted, low-salt and sugar-free brownie treat.

When the dogs of the rich and famous celebrate a birthday, only a specially baked and decorated carob cake from Critter Caterers will do.

Parsons confides she's even baked wedding cakes for celebrity dogs. Another section of the store outfits the bride and groom and the rest of the canine wedding party with lavender and lace and little sequined tuxedos.

Hollywood veterinarian Dr. Bruce Bauersfeld has performed liposuction on dogs, primarily as a necessary medical procedure to remove tumor tissue, but also as a cosmetic job for a canine with a bad case of thunder thighs. The doctor says the procedures have not yet become commonplace, but remember, we're talking Tinseltown here, so stay tuned.

In nearby Santa Monica, at Natures Grooming and Boutique, for $35 owner Leigh Layne offers a luxury moisturizing dog bath that is followed by a choice of four different hypoallergenic rinses and fluffing off with huge towels. Other customers choose a dye job for their poodle in shades of pink, blue and purple. One owner requested that Layne shave little rosebuds into the pet's fur.

Not to be outdone, the proprietors of Animal Inns of America will pick up Spot in a limo and take him to one of their Royal Suites featuring two beds – one for his human valet – along with videotapes of doggy favorite movies or piped-in music.

Doggy drive-thru

In Toledo, Ohio, a night on the town for totally spoiled pets begins and ends at the Puppy Hut, a doggy drive-in operated by Jackie Zajac and Sheila Mullan.

These two imaginative animal lovers met while doing volunteer work for the local animal shelter and decided to pool their talents in a business venture that allowed them to focus full-time on their love for dogs.

Surrounding the drive-thru is what the pair named "The Park and Bark" area where owners and their pets can sit at picnic tables while enjoying Rover's special treat from the all-vegetarian menu. The signs on the grass don't say "Keep Off" or "No Dogs Allowed." Instead they read: "Piles and Puddles Forgiven." Just how much friendlier can you get?

At the Puppy Hut, dogs over nine years old get a senior citizen's discount. And, just in case you can't take your dog out for a night on the town, Puppy Hut delivers!

If your kids are off to camp for the summer, why not send the family dog? Well, each year DogGone, a newsletter about fun places to take your pet, lists doggy camps all across the United States where your mutt can be a happy camper.

At the Canine Camp of the Redwoods, in Santa Cruz, California, an example of some of the workshops and activities Spot will attend include hunting and agility training and long walks in the spectacular Pacific woods.

In Putney, Vermont, at Camp Gone to the Dogs, pooches are entertained with doggy softball games, costume parades and even a bathing suit contest.

A survey taken not long ago by the Hotel Association of New York revealed that the pet that most often accompanies guests at the poshest of those establishments is the dog.

Puttin' on the Ritz

Some of the celebrity dogs who've stayed in the grander lodgings such as the Ritz-Carlton, have demanded – and gotten – service every bit as hoity-toity as visiting royalty.

Lassie, for example, enjoyed Evian water in her crystal dish while staying at the Ritz and dined on patties of choice veal and beef prepared especially for the TV and movie star in that hotel's world-famous kitchen.

In St. Louis, Missouri, dog owners who don't want their pet to have to stay home alone during the day drop them off each morning at Kennelwood Village, a day-care center for dogs.

While there, they're free to dog paddle about in a heated pool – with a lifeguard – or catch a little therapy in the whirlpool.

On an average day, as many as a hundred dogs are dropped off by owners who definitely think of their pets as part of the family, says Kennelwood manager Judy Bremer-Taxman. She goes on to say:

"Mommies and daddies drop their pets off in the morning and pick them up at night. People find it nice to come home at night and find their pup is as exhausted as they are."

A friend
till the end

When the relationship between us and our canine friends at last comes to an end, the respect we have for our pet as part of the family is often shown in many loving ways. More and more Americans are choosing to have a memorial service for their departed companion and a burial that can range from the simple to the lavish.

In Elkridge, Maryland, pet cemetery operator William Green says the average cost of service and burial is around $500, depending on whether the family chooses to have their pet embalmed. Small hardwood caskets, elegantly lined, remain open for a final viewing if the owner wishes.

At Christmas, the graves of dogs at Los Angeles Pet Memorial Park are often decorated with trees and other holiday ornaments by owners who still want to feel united with their departed pet.

According to Julie Hurley: "About 60 percent of the

graves out here are covered with flowers every week and during the holidays people put Christmas trees on the graves with lights and everything."

The oldest operating pet burial place in America is Hartsdale Canine Cemetery in New York state. Director Edward Martin says people who pay that final tribute to a beloved dog aren't odd, but are simply acting on those deep feelings science now admits we hold for pets:

"Many, many people who don't have pets think it's a bizarre way to spend money, but we find that most of the people who come here are just average. The thought of just throwing their pet away isn't acceptable to them. If a dog has shared an important part of your life with you, it isn't hard to understand those feelings," Martin says.

"PUP-POURRI" OF DOG TRIVIA

Dogs laugh, but they laugh with their tails.

Max Eastman

Wouldn't you just love to be smarter than your neighbor, or better yet – your vet – when it comes to little-known facts about dogs?

Here's a whole doggy bag of canine trivia sure to make you the top dog at any cocktail party or backyard barbecue when the topic turns to pooches:

🦴 **Cocker spaniels were first bred in Spain as long as 600 years ago. The "Span" in spaniel is your first clue. "Cocker" comes from the fact that these long-eared darlings were trained by noble Spaniards to flush out woodcocks, a quail-sized fowl the Spanish greatly enjoyed on their dinner tables.**

🦴 Pekingese pooches (that's right, Peking as in China) were once a national Chinese treasure and only royal families were allowed to possess the cute little mops. So prized were these dogs, that the death penalty was the punishment for anyone crazy enough to try to smuggle one from the walled kingdom.

However, leave it to the brave British to do just that. They took off with five of the royal pups during the Boxer Rebellion in 1900, then sent them off by clipper ship to the homeland where they became an instant hit.

🦴 **If barking is a canine trait that annoys you, the pet for you is the basenji – the only dog in the world that does not bark.**

They were originally part of the kingdom of the ancient Pharaohs of Egypt and nearly became extinct, but luckily a few remained. It was not until the 1930s that these terrier-sized, lovable creatures made their way into the United States. While they do not bark, they do make a sound, which experts describe as something like a cross between a yodel and a laugh.

🦴 Tiny Chihuahuas were once sacred to the Aztecs of Mexico. They are among the smallest of all the canine family. But it was not a job without its perils. History relates that on special religious holidays they were cooked and eaten. They took their name from the region of Mexico where they were first bred – the State of Chihuahua.

🦴 **The greyhound is the only dog named by breed in the Bible. It is mentioned in Proverbs 30:29-31, possibly because it is one of the oldest of all breeds. In ancient Egypt, the greyhound enjoyed the same god-like** status as Anubis, the Lord of the Dead.

Alexander the Great owned a greyhound named Peritas. When Homer returned from his Odyssey, the only one who recognized him was his greyhound, Arugs.

In ancient Rome, Diana, goddess of the hunt is portrayed with slim greyhounds at her side. In the play *Henry V*, Shakespeare immortalized that sleek creature in the line "I see you stand like greyhounds in the slips, straining upon the start..."

🦴 If you are a Doberman pinscher lover and feel safer having that alert guardian standing duty in your digs, you'll be interested to know that the breed of pinscher from which the Doberman evolved was developed by a German tax collector named Ludwig Doberman to snarl on command and look mean.

Ludwig was tired of angry German citizens abusing him when he rapped on the door with the annual tax bill. The year was 1880 and Ludwig knew a good idea when he saw one... Before long he quit the tax-collecting biz and started selling Dobies.

🦴 Legend says that the dogs chosen by Noah to accompany his family on the Ark were a pair of Afghan hounds. Science cannot prove that, but it is certain that Afghans were already a well-established breed at the time the great flood occurred.

🦴 The oldest known remains of dogs found to date were discovered in Idaho. They are estimated to be about 10,500 years old. What dogs were doing in Idaho at that time remains an absolute mystery.

🦴 **The little spikes on today's dog collars once had an important meaning. They were sharp and protruding and protected the dog's vulnerable throat when he was fighting other dogs or hunting animals such as wild boar that ferociously fought back.**

🦴 How does Rover know in a heartbeat that you've got the can opener out and are taking the lid off his favorite food or that you have gone to that secret place (or so you thought) where you have hidden his favorite treat?

For one thing, the hearing ability of dogs is twice that of humans and they are able to pick up high-frequency sounds that reach 40,000 vibrations per second.

Then, of course, there is their incredible sense of smell that scientists say can be as much as one million times more sensitive than ours, depending on the breed. Not surprisingly, the all-time champs at sniffing are bloodhounds, but German shepherds are a close second. Both have more than 200 million smell-sensing cells on their schnozzes.

🦴 **The body temperature of your dog is normal in the range from 101 to 102.5 degrees – measured from the rear, of course, and the time required to get an accurate thermometer reading is a full three minutes.**

🦴 The first dog ever registered as a stud with the prestigious American Kennel Club (AKC) was an English setter named – quite appropriately – Adonis, after the Greek god of beauty. The date was 1878.

🦴 In American history, more presidents of the United States have been dog fanciers than cat owners. Our present prez, Bill Clinton, is one of the exceptions, although he hints vaguely that Socks, the family cat, is more or less the pet of daughter Chelsea, rather than himself.

Abraham Lincoln enjoyed the company of Jip, a dog he found shivering in the snow on a visit to a Civil War battlefront. Franklin Roosevelt owned two dogs, Fala and Tiny, and little John and Caroline Kennedy romped with three pooches – Charley, Shannon and Wolf.

The all-time champ, however, was our first chief executive, George Washington, who kept a whole passel of dogs at his working plantation at Mt. Vernon. If you'd like to give one of your dogs a name that George used, try Captain, Cloe, Forester, Lady, Mopsey, Rover, Taster and Tipler.

President Calvin Coolidge had, as his favorite pets, two tiny Chinese Chow-Chow dogs named Tiny Tim and Blackberry. The Chow-Chow's name came from the pidgin-English term "chow-chow" which meant "a little bit of everything."

🦴 President Clinton may not own a dog, but the man who will be his rival in the next presidential election does. According to Senator Bob Dole, he first got himself a pooch after hearing some no-nonsense advice from another U.S. President, Harry S. Truman. "Harry Truman said that if you want a friend in politics, get a dog," Senator Dole says.

🦴 **A dog by any other name may still be the same dog. For example, while the Germans gave the name *dachshund* to the incredibly short-legged creature they admired for his keen scenting abilities and eagerness to hunt crop-damaging badgers, the French call the same animal a *basset* (not to be confused with the basset hound we know here). The Swiss have given it the jaw-breaking name *niederlaufhund*.**

🦴 It may not sound like it to you, but the official description of the baying of a pack of fox or coon hounds in pursuit of their quarry is "music" according to those who follow those sports. Dogs that won't stop baying even when the hunt is over are called "babblers."

🦴 **And, if someone tells you your dog is "corky," don't take offense. It is another dog term that means your pet is lively and alert.**

🦴 The term "foxy" however, doesn't mean you've got the cutest female dog in town – it's the rule-book way of saying the dog has a short fore-face and pointed nose, like her cousin the fox.

🦴 **You may know that the collie is of Scottish origin and one of the most intelligent and useful breeds of animals. But do you know why they were given their name?**

History reports these dogs borrowed the name from the animals they were used to guard and herd, a mountain-climbing breed of still mostly wild sheep called the colley. Just incidentally, the original breeds of collie were nearly all black. It wasn't until years later through interbreeding that they took on that "Lassie" look with which we associate them today.

🦴 The puppy you brought home had 23 "baby" teeth. Full grown, your pet will usually have 23 permanent choppers, although some breeds, because of smaller jaw size, may have a few less.

🦴 Why do we call the hottest days of the summer "dog days?" Because the ancient Romans did.

Their reason? It was part of their religious belief that during the period from July 3 to August 11, Sirus the Dog Star, the brightest constellation in the northern hemisphere added its celestial heat to that of the sun, creating extra heat that made their world swelter.